6/18/21   1-00

to _____

from _____

The Way
To Happiness

The Way To Happiness

BRIDGE PUBLICATIONS, INC.

Published by Bridge Publications, Inc., 1414 N. Catalina St., Los Angeles, CA 90027.
Library of Congress Card Number 81-50592. ISBN 0-88404-173-5
Printed in the United States of America.

How to Use This Book.

You, of course, wish to help your contacts and friends.

Choose someone whose actions, however remotely, may influence your own survival.

Write the person's name on the top line of the front page of this book.

Write or stamp your own name, as an individual, on the second line of the front page.

Present the person with the book.

Ask the person to read it.[0]

---

0. Words sometimes have several different meanings. The footnote definitions given in this book only give the meaning that the word has as it is used in the text. If you find any words in this book you do not know, look them up in a good dictionary. If you do not, then misunderstandings and possible arguments can arise.

You will find that he or she also is threatened with
the possible misconduct of others.

Give the person several additional copies of this
book (or booklet*) but do not write your name on
them: let the other person write his or hers. Have
the person present these copies to others
that are involved in his or her life.

---

* This book is also published as a small, pocket-sized booklet available in packets of
twelve. See page 266 for details.

By continuing to do this you will greatly enhance your own survival potential and theirs.

This is a way toward a much safer and happier life for you and others.

Why I Gave You This Book.

Your

survival[1]

is

important

to

me.

---

1. Survival: The act of remaining alive, of continuing to exist, of being alive.

Happiness.[2]

True joy and happiness are valuable.

If one does not survive, no joy and no happiness are obtainable.

---

2. Happiness: A condition or state of well-being, contentment, pleasure; joyful, cheerful, untroubled existence; the reaction to having nice things happen to one.

Trying to survive in a chaotic,[3] dishonest and
generally immoral[4] society is difficult.

Any individual or group seeks to obtain from life
what pleasure and freedom from pain
that he or they can.

---

3. Chaotic: Having the character or nature of total disorder or confusion.

4. Immoral: Not moral; not following good practices of behavior; not doing right; lacking any idea of proper conduct.

Your own survival can be threatened by the bad actions of others around you.

Your own happiness can be turned to tragedy and sorrow by the dishonesty and misconduct of others.

I am sure you can think of instances of this actually happening. Such wrongs reduce one's survival and impair one's happiness.

You are important to other people. You are listened to. You can influence others.

The happiness or unhappiness of others you could name is important to you.

Without too much trouble, using this book, you can help them survive and lead happier lives.

While no one can guarantee that anyone else can be happy, their chances of survival and happiness can be improved. And with theirs, yours will be.

It is in your power to point the way to a less dangerous and happier life.

Take Care of Yourself.

1-1. Get care when you are ill. When they are ill, even with communicable diseases, people often do not isolate themselves or seek proper treatment. This, as you can easily see, tends to put you at risk. Insist that when someone is ill that he or she takes the proper precautions and gets proper care.

1-2. Keep your body clean. People who do not bathe or wash their hands regularly can carry germs. They put you at risk. You are well within your rights to insist that people bathe regularly and wash their hands. It is inevitable that one gets dirty working or exercising. Get them to clean up afterwards.

1-3. Preserve your teeth. If one brushed one's teeth after every meal, it has been said that one would not suffer tooth decay. This, or chewing gum after each meal, goes far toward defending others from oral diseases and bad breath. Suggest to others that they preserve their teeth.

1-4. Eat properly. People who do not eat properly are not of much help to you or themselves. They tend to have a low energy level. They are sometimes ill-tempered. They become ill more easily. It doesn't require strange diets to eat properly but it does require that one eats nourishing food regularly.

1-5. Get rest. Although many times in life one has to work beyond normal sleep periods, a person's general failure to get proper rest can make him or her a burden to others. Tired people are not alert. They can make mistakes. They have accidents. Just when you need them they can dump the whole workload on one. They put others at risk. Insist that people who do not get proper rest do so.

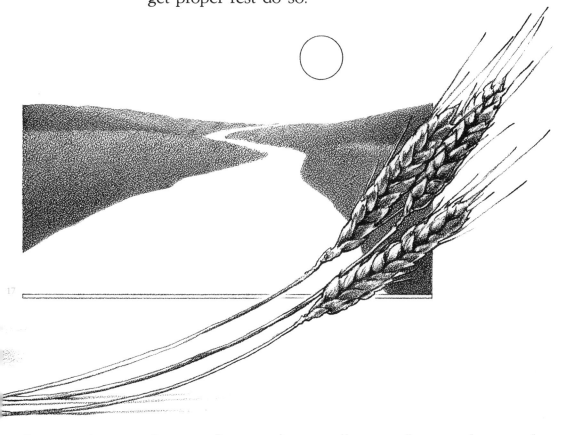

Be Temperate.[5]

2-1. Do not take harmful drugs. People who take drugs do not always see the real world in front of them. They are not really *there*. On a highway, in casual contact, in a home, they can be very dangerous to you. People mistakenly believe they "feel better" or "act better" or are "only happy" when on drugs. This is just another delusion. Sooner or later the drugs will destroy them physically. Discourage people from taking drugs. When they are doing so, encourage them to seek help in getting off them.

---

5. Temperate: Not going to extremes; not overdoing things; controlling one's cravings.

2-2. Do not take alcohol to excess. People who take alcohol are not alert. It impairs their ability to react even when it seems to them they are more alert because of it. Alcohol has some medicinal value. It can be grossly overestimated. Don't let anyone who has been drinking drive you in a car or fly you in a plane. Drinking can take lives in more ways than one. A little liquor goes a long way; don't let too much of it wind up in unhappiness or death.

Deter[6] people from excessive drinking.

---

6. Deter: To prevent or discourage.

*Observing the preceding points, one becomes
more physically able to enjoy life.*

Don't Be Promiscuous.[7]

Sex is the means by which the race projects itself into the future through children and the family. A lot of pleasure and happiness can come from sex: nature intended it that way so the race would go on. But, misused or abused, it carries with it heavy penalties and punishments: nature seems to have intended it that way also.

7. Promiscuous: Casual, random sexual relations.

3-1. Be faithful to your sexual partner. Unfaithfulness on the part of a sexual partner can heavily reduce one's survival. History and the newspapers carry floods of instances of the violence of human passions aroused by unfaithfulness. "Guilt" is the milder evil. Jealousy and vengeance are the greater monsters: one never knows when they will cease to sleep. It is all very well to speak of "being civilized" and "uninhibited" and "understanding"; no talk will mend ruined lives. A "feeling of guilt" is nowhere near as sharp as a knife in the back or ground glass in the soup.

Additionally, there is the question of health. If you do not insist upon faithfulness from a sexual partner, you lay yourself open to disease. For a very brief period, it was said that sexual diseases were all under control. This is not now the case, if it ever was. Incurable strains of such diseases now exist.

The problems of sexual misbehavior are not new. The powerful religion of Buddhism in India vanished from there in the seventh century. According to its own historians the cause was sexual promiscuity in its monasteries. More modernly, when sexual promiscuity becomes prevalent in an organization, commercial or otherwise, the organization can be seen to fail. No matter how civilized their discussions about it, families shatter in the face of unfaithfulness.

The urge of the moment can become the sorrow of a lifetime. Impress those around you with that and safeguard your own health and pleasure.

Sex is a big step on the way to happiness and joy. There is nothing wrong with it if it is followed with faithfulness and decency.

Love and Help Children.

Today's children will become tomorrow's civilization.
Bringing a child into the world today is a little bit
like dropping one into a tiger's cage. Children can't
handle their environment[8] and they have
no real resources. They need love and
help to make it.

---

8. Environment: One's surroundings; the material things around one; the area one lives
in; the living things, objects, spaces and forces with which one lives whether close to or
far away.

It is a delicate problem to discuss. There are almost as many theories on how to raise a child or not
raise him as there are parents. Yet if one does it
incorrectly much grief can result and one may even
complicate his or her own later years. Some try to
raise children the way they were themselves raised,
others attempt the exact opposite, many hold to an
idea that children should just be let grow on their
own. None of these guarantee success. The last

method is based on a materialistic[9] idea that the development of the child parallels the evolutionary[10] history of the race; that in some magical way, unexplained, the "nerves" of the child will "ripen" as he or she grows older and the result will be a moral, well-behaving adult. Although the theory is disproven with ease—simply by noticing the large criminal population whose nerves somehow did not ripen—it is a lazy way to raise children and achieves some popularity. It doesn't take care of your civilization's future or your older years.

---

9. Materialistic: The opinion that only physical matter exists.

10. Evolutionary: Related to a very ancient theory that all plants and animals developed from simpler forms and were shaped by their surroundings rather than being planned or created.

A child is a little bit like a blank slate. If you write the wrong things on it, it will say the wrong things. But, unlike a slate, a child can begin to do the writing: the child tends to write what has been written already. The problem is complicated by the fact that, while most children are capable of great decency, a few are born insane and today, some are even born as drug addicts: but such cases are an unusual few.

It does no good just to try to "buy" the child with an overwhelm of toys and possessions or to smother and protect the child: the result can be pretty awful.

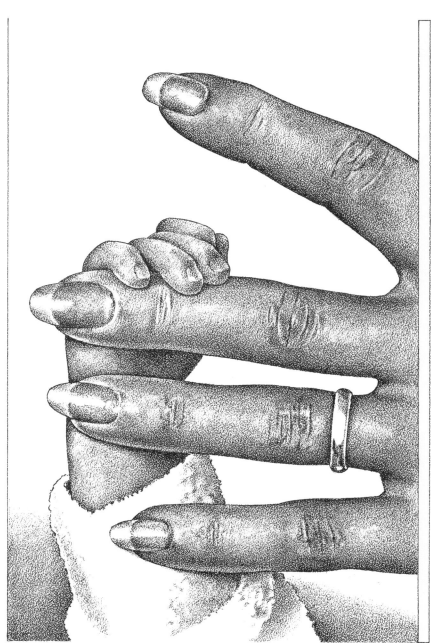

H A P P I N E S S

One has to make up his mind what he is trying to get the child to become. This is modified by several things: a) what the child basically *can* become due to inherent makeup and potential; b) what the child, himself, really wants to become; c) what one wants the child to become; d) the resources available. But remember that whatever these all add up to, the child will *not* survive well unless he or she eventually becomes self-reliant and *very* moral.[11] Otherwise the end product is likely to be a liability to everyone including the child.

11. Moral: Able to know right from wrong in conduct; deciding and acting from that understanding.

Whatever is one's affection for the child, remember that the child cannot survive well in the long run if he or she does not have his or her feet put on the way to survival. It will be no accident if the child goes wrong: the contemporary society is tailor-made for a child's failure.

It will help enormously if you obtain a child's understanding of and agreement to follow the precepts[12] contained in this book.

---

12. Precepts: Rules or statements advising or laying down a principle or principles or a course of action regarding conduct; directions meant as a rule or rules for conduct.

What does have a workability is simply to try to be the child's friend. It is certainly true that a child needs friends. Try to find out what a child's problem really is and without crushing their own solutions, try to help solve them. Observe them—and this applies even to babies. Listen to what children tell you about their lives. Let *them* help—if you don't, they become overwhelmed with a sense of obligation[13] which they then must repress.

---

13. Obligation: The condition or fact of owing another something in return for things, favors or services received.

It will help the child enormously if you obtain understanding of and agreement to this way to happiness and get him or her to follow it. It could have an enormous effect on the child's survival—and yours.

A child factually does not do well without love. Most children have an abundance of it to return.

The way to happiness has on its route the loving and the helping of children from babyhood to the brink of adult life.

38

Honor[14] and Help Your Parents.

From a child's point of view, parents are sometimes hard to understand.

There are differences between generations. But truthfully, this is no barrier. When one is weak, it is a temptation to take refuge in subterfuges and lies: it is this which builds the wall.

---

14. Honor: To show respect for; to treat with deference and courtesy.

Children *can* reconcile their differences with their parents. Before any shouting begins, one can at least try to talk it over quietly. If the child is frank and honest, there cannot help but be an appeal that will reach. It is often possible to attain a compromise[15] where both sides now understand and can agree. It is not always easy to get along with others but one should try.

---

15. Compromise: A settlement of differences in which each side gives in on some point while retaining others and reaching a mutual agreement thereby.

One cannot overlook the fact that almost always,
parents are acting from a very strong desire to do
what they believe to be best for the child.

Children are indebted to their parents for their upbringing—if the parents did so. While some parents are so fiercely independent that they will accept no return on the obligation, it is nevertheless true that there often comes a time when it is the turn of the younger generation to care for their parents.

In spite of all, one must remember that they are the only parents one has. And as such, no matter what, one should honor them and help them.

The way to happiness includes being on good terms
with one's parents or those who brought one up.

Set a Good Example.[16]

There are many people one influences.[17]
The influence[18] can be good
or it can be bad.

If one conducts his life to keep these
recommendations, one is setting
a good example.

Others around one cannot help but be influenced
by this, no matter what they say.

---

16. Example: Someone or something worthy of imitation or duplication; a pattern,
a model.

17. Influences: Has an effect upon.

18. Influence: The resulting effect.

Anyone trying to discourage you is trying to do so because they factually mean you harm or are seeking to serve their own ends. Down deep, they will respect you.

Your own survival chances will be bettered in the long run since others, influenced, will become less of a threat. There are other benefits.

Don't discount the effect you can achieve on others simply by mentioning these things and setting a good example in your own right.

*The way to happiness requires that one set
a good example for others.*

Seek to Live with the Truth.[19]

False data can cause one to make stupid mistakes. It can even block one from absorbing true data.

One can solve the problems of existence only when he has true data.

If those around one lie to him or her, one is lead into making errors and his survival potential is reduced.

---

19. Truth: That which agrees with the facts and observations; logical answers resulting from looking over all the facts and data; a conclusion based on evidence uninfluenced by desire, authority or prejudice; an inevitable (unavoidable) fact no matter how arrived at.

False data can come from many sources:
academic, social, professional.

Many want you to believe things just to
suit their own ends.

What is *true* is what is true for *you*.

No one has any right to force data on you and
command you to believe it or else.
If it is not true for you,
it isn't true.

Think your own way through things, accept what is
true for you, discard the rest. There is nothing
unhappier than one who tries to live
in a chaos of lies.

7-1. Do not tell harmful lies.[20] Harmful lies are the product of fear, malice and envy. They can drive people to acts of desperation. They can ruin lives. They create a kind of trap into which the teller and the target can both fall. Interpersonal and social chaos can result. Many wars began because of harmful lies.

One should learn to detect them and reject them.

---

20. Lies: False statements or pieces of information deliberately presented as being true; a falsehood; anything meant to deceive or give a wrong impression.

7-2. Do not bear false witness. There are considerable penalties connected with swearing or testifying to untrue "facts." It is called "perjury": it has heavy penalties.

The way to happiness lies along the road to truth.

Do Not Murder.[21]

Most races, from the most ancient times to the present, have prohibited murder and punished it heavily. Sometimes this has been broadened to say, "Thou shalt not kill," when a later translation of the same work has found it to read "Thou shalt not murder."

21. Murder: The unlawful killing of one (or more) human being(s) by another, especially with malice aforethought (intending to do so before the act).

There is a considerable difference between these two words *kill* and *murder.* A prohibition against all killing would rule out self-defense; it would tend to make it illegal to handle a serpent coiling to strike the baby; it would put a race on a diet of vegetables. I am sure you can see many illustrations of the difficulties raised by a prohibition against all killing.

"Murder" is another thing entirely. By definition it means, "The unlawful killing of one (or more) human being(s) by another, especially with malice aforethought." One can easily see that in this age of violent weaponry, murder would be all too easy. One could not exist in a society where oneself or one's family or friends were at the mercy of some who went about casually taking lives.

Murder justly bears the highest priority in social prevention and retaliation.

The stupid, the evil and the insane seek to solve their real or imagined problems with murder. And they have been known to do it for no reason at all.

Get behind any demonstrably effective program that handles this threat to mankind and push. Your own survival could depend upon it.

The way to happiness does not include murdering your friends, your family, or yourself being murdered.

Don't Do Anything Illegal.

"Illegal acts" are those which are prohibited by
official rules or law. They are the product of rulers,
legislative bodies and judges. They are usually written down in law codes. In a well-ordered society,
these are published and made known generally. In
a cloudy—and often crime-ridden—society one has
to consult an attorney or be specially trained to
know them all; such a society will tell one
that "ignorance is no excuse
for breaking the law."

Any member of society, however, has a responsibility, whether young or old, for knowing what that society considers to be an "illegal act." People can be asked, libraries exist where they can be looked up.

An "illegal act" is not disobedience to some casual order like "go to bed." It is an action which, if done, can result in punishment by the courts and state: being pilloried[22] by the state propaganda[23] machine, being fined and even by being imprisoned.

---

22. Pilloried: Exposed to ridicule, public contempt, scorn or abuse.

23. Propaganda: Spreading ideas, information or rumor to further one's own cause and/or injure that of another, often without regard to truth; the act of putting lies in the press or on radio and TV so that when a person comes to trial he will be found guilty; the action of falsely damaging a person's reputation so he will not be listened to. Propagandist: A person or group who does, makes or practices propaganda.

When one does something illegal, small or large, one is laid open to an attack by the state. It does not matter whether one is caught or not, when one does an illegal act, one has weakened one's defenses.

Almost any worthwhile thing one is trying to accomplish often can be done in perfectly legal ways. The "illegal" route is a dangerous and time-wasting shortcut. Imagined "advantages" in committing illegal acts usually turn out not to be worth it.

The state and government tends to be a rather unthinking machine. It exists and works on laws and codes of laws. It is geared to strike down through its channels at illegality. As such it can be an implacable[24] enemy; adamant[25] on the subject of "illegal acts." The rightness and wrongness of things do not count in the face of laws and codes of laws. Only the laws count.

---

24. Implacable: Not open to being quieted, soothed or pleased; remorseless; relentless.

25. Adamant: Hard; not giving in; unyielding; something which won't break, insistent; refusing any other opinion; surrendering to nothing.

When you realize or discover that those about you are committing "illegal acts," you should do what you can to discourage it. You yourself, not even a party to it, can yet suffer because of it. The firm's accountant falsifies the books: in any resulting commotion, the firm could fail and you could lose your job. Such instances can grossly affect one's own survival.

As a member of any group subject to laws, encourage the clear-cut publication of those laws so they can be known. Support any legal, political effort to reduce, clarify and codify the laws that apply to that group. Adhere to the principle that all men are equal under law: a principle which, in its own time and place—the tyrannical[26] days of aristocracy[27]—was one of the greatest social advances in human history and should not be lost sight of.

---

26. Tyrannical: The use of cruel, unjust and absolute power; crushing; oppressing; harsh; severe.

27. Aristocracy: Government by a few with special privileges, ranks or positions; rule by an elite few who are above the general law; a group who by birth or position are "superior to everybody else" and who can make or apply laws to others but consider that they themselves are not affected by the laws.

See that children and people become informed of what is "legal" and what is "illegal" and make it known, if by as little as a frown, that you do not approve of "illegal acts."

Those who commit them, even when they "get away
with them," are yet weakened before
the might of the state.

The way to happiness does not include
the fear of being found out.

Support a Government Designed and Run for All the People.

Unscrupulous and evil men and groups can usurp
the power of government and use it
to their own ends.

Government organized and conducted solely for
self-interested individuals and groups gives the
society a short life span. This imperils the survival
of everyone in the land; it even imperils those
who attempt it. History is full of
such governmental deaths.

Opposition to such governments usually just brings on more violence.

But one can raise his voice in caution when such abuses are abroad. And one need not actively support such a government; doing nothing illegal, it is

yet possible, by simply withdrawing one's coopera-
tion, to bring about an eventual reform. Even as
this is being written there are several governments
in the world that are failing only because their
people express their silent disagreement by simply
not cooperating. These governments are at risk:
any untimely wind of mischance
could blow them over.

On the other hand, where a government is obviously working hard for all its people, rather than for some special interest group or insane dictator, one should support it to the limit.

There is a subject called "government." In schools they mainly teach "civics" which is merely how the current organization is put together. The real subject, "government," goes under various headings: political economy, political philosophy, political power, etc. The whole subject of "government" and how to govern can be quite precise, almost a technical science. If one is interested in having a better government, one that does not cause trouble, one should suggest it be taught at earlier ages in schools; one can also read up on it: it is not a very difficult subject if you look up the big words.

It is, after all, the people and their own opinion leaders who sweat and fight and bleed for their country—a government cannot bleed, it cannot even smile: it is just an idea men have. It is the individual person who is alive—*you.*

The way to happiness is hard to travel when shadowed with the oppression of tyranny. A benign government, designed and run for all the people, has been known to smooth the way: when such occurs, it deserves support.

Do Not Harm a Person of Good Will.[28]

Despite the insistence of evil men that all men are evil, there are many good men around and women, too. You may have been fortunate enough to know some.

---

28. Good will: Bearing or attitude toward others; disposition; traditionally, "men of good will" means those who mean well toward their fellows and work to help them.

Factually, the society runs on men and women of good will. Public workers, opinion leaders, those in the private sector who do their jobs are, in the great majority, people of good will. If they weren't, they long since would have ceased to serve.

Such people are easy to attack: their very decency
prevents them from overprotecting themselves.
Yet the survival of most of the individuals
in a society depends upon them.

The violent criminal, the propagandist,[23] the sensation-seeking media all tend to distract one's attention from the solid, everyday fact that the society would not run at all were it not for the individuals of good will. As they guard the street, counsel the children, take the temperatures, put out the fires and speak good sense in quiet voices, one is apt to overlook the fact that people of good will are the ones that keep the world going and man alive upon this Earth.

---

23. Propagandist: A person or group who does, makes or practices propaganda. Propaganda: Spreading ideas, information or rumor to further one's own cause and/or injure that of another, often without regard to truth; the act of putting lies in the press or on radio and TV so that when a person comes to trial he will be found guilty; the action of falsely damaging a person's reputation so he will not be listened to.

Yet such can be attacked and strong measures
should be advocated and taken to defend them and
keep them from harm, for your own survival
and that of your family and friends
depends upon them.

*The way to happiness is far more easily followed
when one supports people of good will.*

Safeguard[29] and Improve Your Environment.

12-1. Be of good appearance. It sometimes does not occur to some individuals—as they do not have to spend their days looking at themselves—that they form part of the scenery and appearance of others. And some do not realize that they are judged by others on the basis of their appearance.

---

29. Safeguard: Prevent from being harmed; protect.

While clothes can be expensive, soap and the other tools of self-care are not that hard to obtain. The techniques are sometimes difficult to dig up but can be evolved.

In some societies, when they are barbaric or become very degraded, it can even be the fashion to be a public eyesore. Actually it is a symptom of a lack of self-respect.

Exercising and working, one can become very messed up. But this does not rule out getting cleaned up. And as an example, some European and English workmen manage a style of appearance even when working. Some of the better athletes, one notices, look good despite being wringing wet with sweat.

An environment disfigured with unkempt people
can have a subtle, depressing effect
on one's morale.[30]

---

30. Morale: The mental and emotional attitude of an individual or a group; sense of
well-being; willingness to get on with it; a sense of common purpose.

Encourage people around you to look good by complimenting them when they do or even gently helping them with their problems when they don't. It could improve their self-regard and their morale as well.

12-2. Take care of your own area. When people mess up their own possessions and area, it can slop over into your own.

When people seem to be incapable of caring for their own things and places, it is a symptom of their feeling that they don't really belong there and don't really own their own things. When young, the things they were "given" had too many cautions and strings attached or were taken away from them by brothers, sisters or parents. And they possibly did not feel welcome.

The possessions, the rooms and work spaces, the vehicles of such people advertise that they are not really the property of anyone. Worse, a sort of rage against possessions can sometimes be seen. Vandalism[31] is a manifestation of it: the house or car "nobody owns" is soon ruined.

---

31. Vandalism: The willful and malicious destruction of public or private property, especially anything beautiful or artistic.

Those who build and try to maintain low-income housing are often dismayed by the rapidity with which ruin can set in. The poor, by definition, own little or nothing. Harassed in various ways, they also come to feel they do not belong.

But whether rich or poor, and for whatever reason, people who do not take care of their possessions and places can cause disorder to those about them. I am sure you can think of such instances.

Ask such people what they really do own in life and if they really belong where they are and you will receive some surprising answers.
And help them a great deal, too.

The skill of organizing possessions and places can be taught. It can come as a new idea to someone that an item, when picked up and used, should be put back in the same place so it can be found again: some spend half their time just looking for things. A little time spent getting organized can pay off in speeded work: it is not the waste of time some believe.

To protect your own possessions and places, get others to take care of theirs.

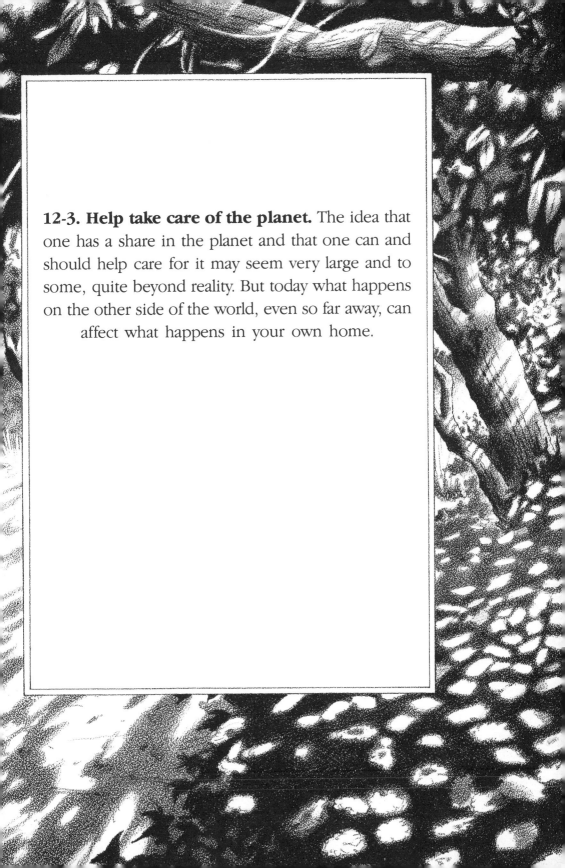

12-3. Help take care of the planet. The idea that one has a share in the planet and that one can and should help care for it may seem very large and to some, quite beyond reality. But today what happens on the other side of the world, even so far away, can affect what happens in your own home.

Recent discoveries by space probes to Venus have
shown that our own world could be deteriorated to
a point where it would no longer support life. And it
possibly could happen in one's own lifetime.

Cut down too many forests, foul too many rivers
and seas, mess up the atmosphere and we have had
it. The surface temperature can go roasting hot,
the rain can turn to sulfuric acid.
All living things could die.

One can ask, "Even if that were true, what could I do about it?" Well, even if one were simply to frown when people do things to mess up the planet, one would be doing something about it. Even if one only had the opinion that it was just not a good thing to wreck the planet and mentioned that opinion, one would be doing something.

Care of the planet begins in one's own front yard. It extends through the area one travels to get to school or work. It covers such places as where one picnics or goes on vacation. The litter which messes up the terrain and water supply, the dead brush which invites fire, these are things one need not contribute to and which, in otherwise idle moments, one can do something about. Planting a tree may seem little enough but it is something.

In some countries, old people, the unemployed, do not just sit around and go to pieces: they are used to care for the gardens and parks and forests, to pick up the litter and add some beauty to the world. There is no lack of resources to take care of the planet. They are mainly ignored. One notes that the Civilian Conservation Corps in the U.S., organized in the 1930s to absorb the energies of unemployed officers and youth, was one of the few, if not the only project of that depressed era that created far more wealth for the state than was expended. It reforested large areas and did other valuable things that cared for the U.S. part of the planet. One notes that the C.C.C. no longer exists. One can do as little as add one's opinion that such projects are worthwhile and support opinion leaders and organizations that carry on environmental work.

There is no lack of technology. But technology and its application cost money. Money is available when sensible economic policies, policies which do not penalize everyone, are followed.
Such policies exist.

There are many things people can do to help take care of the planet. They begin with the idea that one should. They progress by suggesting to others that they should.

Man has reached the potential capacity to destroy
the planet. He must be pushed on up to the
capability and actions of saving it. It is,
after all, what we're standing on.

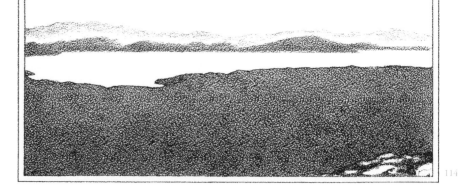

If others do not help safeguard and improve the environment, the way to happiness could have no roadbed to travel on at all.

Do Not Steal.

When one does not respect the ownership of things,
his own possessions and property are at risk.

A person, who for one reason or another has been
unable to honestly accumulate possessions, can
pretend that nobody owns anything anyway.
But don't try to steal his shoes!

A thief sows the environment with mysteries: what
happened to this, what happened to that?
A thief causes trouble far in excess
of the value of things stolen.

Faced with the advertising of desirable goods, torn by the incapability of doing anything valuable enough to acquire possessions or simply driven by an impulse, those who steal imagine they are acquiring something valuable at low cost. But that is the difficulty: the cost. The actual price to the thief is high beyond belief. The greatest robbers in history paid for their loot by spending their lives in wretched hide-outs and prisons with only rare moments of "the good life." No amount of stolen valuables would reward such a horrible fate.

Stolen goods greatly reduce in value: they have to be hidden, they are always a threat to liberty itself. Even in communist states, the thief is sent to prison.

Stealing things is really just an admission that one is not capable enough to make it honestly. Or that one has a streak of insanity. Ask a thief which one it is: it's either one or the other.

*The road to happiness cannot be traveled
with stolen goods.*

Be Worthy of Trust.

Unless one can have confidence in the reliability of
those about one, he, himself, is at risk. When those
he counts upon let him down, his own life can
become disordered and even his own survival
can be put at risk.

Mutual trust is the firmest building block in human
relationships. Without it, the whole structure
comes down.

Trustworthiness is a highly esteemed commodity. When one has it, one is considered valuable. When one has lost it, one may be considered worthless.

One should get others around one to demonstrate it and earn it. They will become much more valuable to themselves and others thereby.

14-1. Keep your word once given. When one gives an assurance or promise or makes a sworn intention, one must make it come true. If one says he is going to do something, he should do it. If he says he is not going to do something, he should not do it.

One's regard for another is based, in no small degree, on whether or not the person keeps his or her word. Even parents, for instance, would be surprised at the extent they drop in the opinion of their children when a promise is not kept.

People who keep their word are trusted and admired. People who do not are regarded like garbage. Those who break their word often never get another chance.

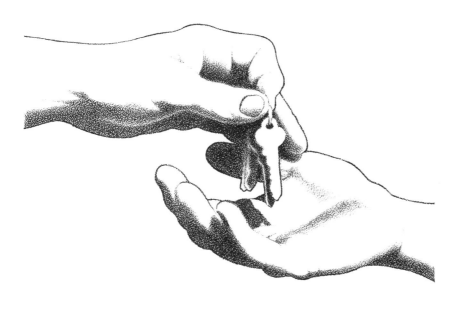

A person who does not keep his word can soon find himself entangled and trapped in all manner of "guarantees" and "restrictions" and can even find himself shut off from normal relations with others. There is no more thorough self-exile from one's fellows than to fail to keep one's promises once made.

One should never permit another to give his or her word lightly. And one should insist that when a promise is made, it must be kept. One's own life can become very disordered in trying to associate with people who do not keep their promises. It is not a casual matter.

The way to happiness is much, much easier to travel with people one can trust.

Fulfill Your Obligations.[32]

In going through life, one inevitably incurs obligations. Factually, one is born with certain obligations and they tend to accumulate thereafter. It is no novel or new idea that one owes his parents a debt for bringing one into the world, for raising one. It is a credit to parents that they don't push it any harder than they do. But it is an obligation, nevertheless: even the child feels it. And as life continues to run its course, one accumulates other obligations—
to other persons, to friends, to society
and even the world.

---

32. Obligation: The state, fact or condition of being indebted to another for a special service or favor received; a duty, contract, promise or any other social, moral or legal requirement that binds one to follow or avoid a certain course of action; the sense of owing another.

It is an extreme disservice to a person not to permit him to satisfy or pay off his obligations. No small part of the "revolt of childhood" is caused by others refusing to accept the only "coins" a baby or child or youth has with which to discharge the "weight of obligation": the baby's smiles, the child's fumbling efforts to help, the youth's possible advice or just the effort to be a good son or a good daughter commonly pass unrecognized, unaccepted; they can be ill-aimed, often ill-planned; they fade quickly. Such efforts, when they fail to discharge the enormity of the debt, can be replaced with any number of mechanisms or rationalizations: "One doesn't really owe anything," "I was owed it all in the first place," "I didn't ask to be born," "My parents or guardians are no good" and "Life isn't worth living anyway," to name a few. And yet the obligations continue to pile up.

The "weight of obligation" can be a crushing burden if one can see no way to discharge it. It can bring about all manner of individual or social disorders. When it cannot be discharged, those who are owed, often unwittingly, find themselves targets for the most unlooked-for reactions.

One can help a person who finds himself in the
dilemma of unpaid obligations and debt by simply
going over with him or her *all* the obligations they
have incurred and have not fulfilled—moral, social
and financial—and working out some way to
discharge *all* of them the person
feels are still owed.

One should accept the efforts of a child or an adult to pay off non-financial obligations they feel they may owe. One should help bring about some mutually agreeable solution to the discharge of financial ones.

Discourage a person from incurring more
obligations than it is possible
for him or her to actually
discharge or repay.

The way to happiness is very hard to travel when one is burdened with the weight of obligations which one is owed or which he has not discharged.

Be Industrious.[33]

Work is not always pleasant.

But few are unhappier than those who lead a purposeless, idle and bored existence: children gloom to their mother when they have nothing to do; the low-mindedness of the unemployed, even when they are on "relief"[34] or the "dole"[35] is legendary; the retired man, with nothing further to accomplish in life, perishes from inactivity, as shown by statistics.

---

33. Industrious: Applying oneself with energy to study or work; actively and purposefully getting things done; opposite of being idle and accomplishing nothing.

34. Relief: Goods or money given by a government agency to people because of need or poverty.

35. Dole: The British term for government relief.

Even the tourist, lured by a travel agency's call to
leisure, gives a tour conductor a bad time
if he has nothing for them to do.

Sorrow itself can be eased by simply
getting busy at something.

Morale is boosted to high highs by accomplishment.
In fact, it can be demonstrated that production[36]
is the basis of morale.

---

36. Production: The act of completing something; finishing a task, project or object that
is useful or valuable or simply worth doing or having.

People who are not industrious dump the
workload on those around them.
They tend to burden one.

It is hard to get along with idle people. Aside
from depressing one, they can also
be a bit dangerous.

A workable answer is to persuade such to decide on
some activity and get them busy with it. The most
lasting benefit will be found to arise from work
that leads to actual production.

*The way to happiness is a high road when it includes
industriousness that leads to tangible production.*

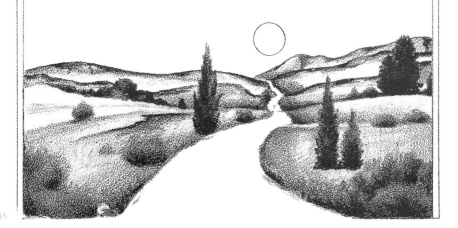

Be Competent.[37]

In an age of intricate equipment and high-speed
machines and vehicles, one's survival and that of
one's family and friends depends in no small
measure upon the general competence
of others.

In the marketplace, in the sciences, the humanities
and in government, incompetence[38] can threaten
the lives and future of the few or the many.

I am sure you can think of many examples of this.

---

37. Competent: Able to do well those things one does; capable; skilled in doing what one
does; measuring up to the demands of one's activities.

38. Incompetence: Lacking adequate knowledge or skill or ability; unskilled; incapable;
subject to making big errors or mistakes; bungling.

Man has always had an impulse to control his fate. Superstition, propitiation of the right gods, ritual dances before the hunt, can all be viewed as efforts, no matter how faint or unavailing, to control destiny.

It was not until he learned to think, to value
knowledge and to apply it with competent skill
that he began to dominate his environment.
The true "gift of heaven" may have been
the potential to be competent.

In common pursuits and activities, man respects
skill and ability. These in a hero or athlete
are almost worshiped.

The test of true competence is the end result.

To the degree that a man is competent, he survives.
To the degree he is incompetent, he perishes.

Encourage the attainment of competence in any worthwhile pursuit. Compliment it and reward it whenever you find it.

Demand high performance standards. The test of a society is whether or not you, your family and friends can live in it safely.

The ingredients of competence include observation, study and practice.

17-1. Look. See what you see, not what someone tells you that you see.

What you observe is what *you* observe. Look at things and life and others directly, not through any cloud of prejudice, curtain of fear or the interpretation of another.

Instead of arguing with others, get them to look. The most flagrant lies can be punctured, the greatest pretenses can be exposed, the most intricate puzzles can be resolved and the most remarkable revelations can occur, simply by gently insisting that someone *look*.

When another finds things almost too confusing
and difficult to bear, when his or her wits are going
around and around, get the person to just
stand back and look.

What they find is usually very obvious when they
see it. Then they can go on and handle things. But
if they don't see it themselves, observe it for
themselves, it may have little reality for them and all
the directives and orders and punishment in the
world will not resolve their muddle.

While one can indicate what direction to look and
suggest that they do look, the conclusions
are up to them.

A child or adult sees what he himself sees and
that is reality for him.

True competence is based on one's own ability to
observe. With that as reality, only then can one
be deft and sure.

17-2. Learn. Has there ever been an instance when
another had some false data about you?
Did it cause you trouble?

This can give you some idea of the havoc false data
can raise. You could also have some
false data about another.

Separating the false from the true
brings about understanding.

There is a lot of false data around. Evil-intentioned
individuals manufacture it to serve their own
purposes. Some of it comes from just plain
ignorance of the facts. It can block
the acceptance of true data.

The main process of learning consists of inspecting the available data, selecting the true from the false, the important from the unimportant and arriving thereby at conclusions one makes and can apply. If one does this, one is well on the way to being competent.

The test of any "truth" is whether it is true for *you*. If, when one has gotten the body of data, cleared up any words in it that one does not fully understand and looked over the scene, it still doesn't seem true, then it isn't true so far as you are concerned. Reject it. And if you like, carry it further and conclude what the truth is for *you*. After all, *you* are the one who is going to have to use it or not use it, think with it or not think with it. If one blindly accepts "facts" or "truths" just because he is told he must, "facts" and "truths" which do not seem true to one, or even false, the end result can be an unhappy one. That is the alley to the trash bin of incompetence.

Another part of learning entails simply committing things to memory—like the spelling of words, mathematical tables and formulas, the sequence of which buttons to push. But even in simple memorizing one has to know what the material is for and how and when to use it.

The process of learning is not just piling data on top of more data. It is one of obtaining new understandings and better ways to do things.

Those who get along in life never really stop studying and learning. The competent engineer keeps up with new ways; the good athlete continually reviews the progress of his sport; any professional keeps a stack of his texts to hand and consults them.

The new model eggbeater or washing machine, the latest year's car all demand some study and learning before they can be competently operated. When people omit it, there are accidents in the kitchen and piles of bleeding wreckage on the highways.

It is a very arrogant fellow who thinks he has
nothing further to learn in life. It is a dangerously
blind individual who cannot shed his prejudices
and false data and supplant them with facts and
truths that can more fittingly assist his own life
and everyone else's.

There are ways to study so that one really learns and can use what one learns. In brief, it consists of having a teacher and/or texts which know what they are talking about, of clearing up every word one does not fully understand, of consulting other references and/or the scene of the subject, of sorting out the false data one might already have and of sifting the false from the true on the basis of what is now true for you. The end result will be certainty and potential competence. It can be, actually, a bright and rewarding experience. Not unlike climbing a treacherous mountain through brambles but coming out on top with a new view of the whole, wide world.

A civilization, to survive, must nurture the habits and abilities to study in its schools. A school is not a place where one puts children to get them out from underfoot during the day. That would be far too expensive for just that. It is not a place where one manufactures parrots. School is where one should learn to study and where children can be prepared to come to grips with reality; to learn to handle it with competence and to be readied to take over tomorrow's world, the world where current adults will be in their later years, middle or old age.

The hardened criminal never learned to learn. Repeatedly the courts seek to teach him that if he commits the crime again he will go back to prison: most of them do commit the same crime again and do go back to prison. Factually, criminals cause more and more laws to be passed. The decent citizen is the one that obeys laws; the criminals, by definition, do not. Criminals cannot learn. Not all the orders and directives and punishments and duress will work upon a being that does not know how to learn and cannot learn.

A characteristic of a government that has gone criminal—as has sometimes happened in history—is that its leaders cannot learn: all records and good sense may tell them that disaster follows oppression; yet it has taken violent revolutions to handle them or a World War II to get rid of a Hitler and those were very unhappy events for mankind. Such did not learn. They revelled in false data. They refused all evidence and truth.

They had to be blown away.

The insane cannot learn. Driven by hidden evil intentions or crushed beyond the ability to reason, facts and truth and reality are far beyond them. They personify false data. They will not or cannot really perceive or learn.

A multitude of personal and social problems arise from the inability or refusal to learn.

The lives of some around you have gone off the rails because they do not know how to study, because they do not learn. You can probably think of some examples.

If one cannot get those around him to study and learn, one's own work can become much harder and even overloaded and one's own survival potential can be greatly reduced.

One can help others study and learn if only by putting in their reach the data they should have. One can help simply by acknowledging what they have learned. One can assist if only by appreciating any demonstrated increase in competence. If one likes, one can do more than that: others can be assisted by helping them, without disputes, to sort out false data; by helping them find and clear up words they have not understood; by helping them find and handle the reasons they do not study and learn.

As life is largely trial and error, instead of coming down on somebody who makes a mistake, find out how come a mistake was made and see if the other can't learn something from it.

Now and then you may surprise yourself by untangling a person's life just by having gotten the person to study and learn. I am sure you can think of many ways. And I think you will find the gentler ones work best. The world is brutal enough already to people who can't learn.

17-3. Practice.[39] Learning bears fruit when it is applied. Wisdom, of course, can be pursued for its own sake: there is even a kind of beauty in it. But, truth told, one never really knows if he is wise or not until he sees the results of trying to apply it.

39. Practice: To exercise or perform repeatedly in order to acquire or polish a skill.

Any activity, skill or profession—ditch digging, law,
engineering, cooking or whatever—no matter how
well studied, collides at last with the acid test:
can one *DO* it? And that doing
requires *practice.*

Movie stunt men who don't practice first get hurt.
So do housewives.

Safety is not really a popular subject. Because it is
usually accompanied by "Be careful" and "Go slow,"
people can feel restraints are being put on them.
But there is another approach: if one is really
practiced, his skill and dexterity is such that he
doesn't have to "be careful" or "go slow." Safe
high speed of motion becomes possible
only with practice.

One's skill and dexterity must be brought up to
match the speed of the age one lives in.
And that is done with practice.

One can train one's body, one's eyes, one's hands and feet until, with practice, they sort of "get to know." One no longer has to "think" to set up the stove or park the car: one just *DOES* it. In any activity, quite a bit of what passes for "talent" is really just *practice*.

Without working out each movement one makes to
do something and then doing it over and over until
one can get it done without even thinking about it
and get it done with speed and accuracy,
one can set the stage for accidents.

Statistics tend to bear out that the least practiced
have the most accidents.

The same principle applies to crafts and professions which mainly use the mind. The lawyer who has not drilled, drilled, drilled on courtroom procedure may not have learned to shift his mental gears fast enough to counter new turns of a case and loses it. An undrilled new stockbroker could lose a fortune in minutes. A green salesman who has not rehearsed selling can starve for lack of sales. The right answer is to practice, practice and practice!

Sometimes one finds that what one has learned he cannot apply. If so, the faults lay with improper study or with the teacher or text. It is one thing to read the directions, it is sometimes another thing entirely to try to apply them.

Now and then, when one is getting nowhere with practice, one has to throw the book away and start from scratch. The field of movie sound recording has been like that: if one followed what recordist texts there have been, one wouldn't get a bird song to sound any better than a foghorn—that is why you can't tell what the actors are saying in some movies. The good sound recordist had to work it all out for himself in order to do his job. But in the same field of the cinema there is a complete reverse of this: several texts on cine lighting are excellent;
if followed exactly, one gets
a beautiful scene.

It is regrettable, particularly in a high-speed technical society, that not all activities are adequately covered with understandable texts. But that should not stop one. When good texts exist, value them and study them well. Where they don't, assemble what data is available, study that and work the rest of it out.

But theory and data blossom only when applied and applied with practice.

One is at risk when those about one do not practice
their skills until they can really DO them. There is
a vast difference between "good enough" and
professional skill and dexterity. The gap
is bridged with practice.

Get people to look, study, work it out and then do
it. And when they have it right, get them to
practice, practice, practice until they
can do it like a pro.

There is considerable joy in skill, dexterity and
moving fast: it can only be done safely with practice.
Trying to live in a high-speed world with
low-speed people is not very safe.

The way to happiness is best traveled
with competent companions.

Respect the Religious Beliefs of Others.

Tolerance is a good cornerstone on which to build human relationships. When one views the slaughter and suffering caused by religious intolerance throughout all the history of man and into modern times, one can see that intolerance is a very nonsurvival activity.

Religious tolerance does not mean one cannot express his own beliefs. It does mean that seeking to undermine or attack the religious faith and beliefs of another has always been a short road to trouble.

Philosophers since the time of ancient Greece have disputed with one another about the nature of God, man and the universe. The opinions of authorities ebb and flow. Just now the philosophies of "mechanism"[40] and "materialism"[41]—dating as far back as Egypt and Greece—are the fad: they seek to assert that all is matter and overlook that, neat as their explanations of evolution may be, they still do not rule out *additional* factors that might be at

---

40. Mechanism: The view that all life is only matter in motion and can be totally explained by physical laws. Advanced by Leucippus and Democritus (460 B.C. to 370 B.C.) who may have gotten it from Egyptian mythology. Upholders of this philosophy felt they had to neglect religion because they could not reduce it to mathematics. They were attacked by religious interests and in their turn attacked religion. Robert Boyle (1627-91) who developed Boyle's Law in physics, refuted it by raising the question as to whether or not nature might have designs such as matter in motion.

41. Materialism: Any one of a family of metaphysical theories which view the universe as consisting of hard objects such as stones, very big or very small. The theories seek to explain away such things as minds by saying they can be reduced to physical things or their motions. Materialism is a very ancient idea. There are other ideas.

work, that might be merely using such things as evolution. They are, today, the "official" philosophies and are even taught in schools. They have their own zealots who attack the beliefs and religions of others: the result can be intolerance and contention.

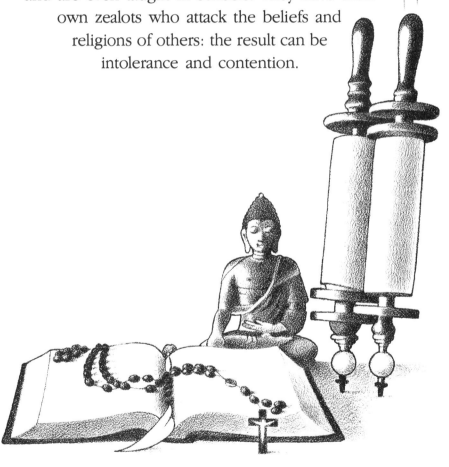

If all the brightest minds since the fifth century B.C. or before have never been able to agree on the subject of religion or antireligion, it is an arena of combat between people that one would do well to stay out of.

In this sea of contention, one bright principle has emerged: the right to believe as one chooses.

"Faith" and "belief" do not necessarily surrender to logic: they cannot even be declared to be illogical. They can be things quite apart.

Any advice one might give another on this subject is safest when it simply asserts the right to believe as one chooses. One is at liberty to hold up his own beliefs for acceptance. One is at risk when he seeks to assault the beliefs of others, much more so when he attacks and seeks to harm others because of their religious convictions.

Man, since the dawn of the species, has taken great consolation and joy in his religions. Even the "mechanist" and "materialist" of today sound much like the priests of old as they spread their dogma.

Men without faith are a pretty sorry lot. They can
even be given something to have faith in.
But when they have religious beliefs,
respect them.

The way to happiness can become contentious when one fails to respect the religious beliefs of others.

Try Not to Do Things to Others That You Would Not Like Them to Do to You.

Among many peoples in many lands for many ages there have been versions of what is commonly called "The Golden Rule."[42] The above is a wording of it that relates to harmful acts.

---

42. "The Golden Rule": Although this is looked upon by Christians as Christian and is found in the New and Old Testaments, many other races and peoples spoke of it. It also appears in the *Analects* of Confucius (fifth and sixth centuries B.C.) who, himself, quoted from more ancient works. It is also found in "primitive" tribes. In one form or another it appears in the ancient works of Plato, Aristotle, Isocrates and Seneca. For thousands of years it has been held by man as a standard of ethical conduct. The versions given in this book are newly worded, however, as in earlier wordings it was thought to be too idealistic to be kept. It is possible to keep this version.

Only a saint could go through life without ever harming another. But only a criminal hurts those around him without a second thought.

Completely aside from feelings of "guilt" or "shame" or "conscience," all of which can be real enough and bad enough, it also happens to be true that the harm one does to others can recoil on oneself.

Not all harmful acts are reversible: one can commit an act against another which cannot be waived aside or forgotten. Murder is such an act. One can work out how severe violation of almost any precept in this book could become an irreversible harmful act against another.

The ruin of another's life can wreck one's own. Society reacts—the prisons and the insane asylums are stuffed with people who harmed their fellows. But there are other penalties: whether one is caught or not, committing harmful acts against others, particularly when hidden, can cause one to suffer severe changes in his attitudes toward others and himself, all of them unhappy ones. The happiness and joy of life depart.

This version of "The Golden Rule" is also useful as a test. When one persuades someone to apply it, the person can attain a reality on what a harmful act *is*.

It answers for one what *harm* is. The philosophic question concerning *wrongdoing,* the argument of what is wrong is answered at once on a personal basis: would you not like that to happen to you? No? Then it must be a harmful action and from society's viewpoint, a wrong action. It can awaken social consciousness. It can then let one work out what one should do and what one should not do.

In a time when some feel no restraint from doing harmful acts, the survival potential of the individual sinks to a very low ebb.

If you can persuade people to apply this, you will have given them a precept by which they can evaluate their own lives and for some, opened the door to let them rejoin the human race.

The way to happiness is closed to those who do not restrain themselves from committing harmful acts.

Try to Treat Others As You Would Want Them to Treat You.

This is a positive version of "The Golden Rule."

Don't be surprised if someone seems to resent
being told to "be good." But the resentment may
not come at all at the idea of "being good."
It may be because the person factually has
a misunderstanding of what it means.

One can get into a lot of conflicting opinions and confusions about what "good behavior" might be. One might never have grasped—even if the teacher did—why he or she was given the grade received for "conduct." One might even have been given or assumed false data concerning it: "Children should be seen and not heard," "Being good means being inactive."

However, there is a way to clear it all up to one's complete satisfaction.

In all times and in most places, mankind has looked up to and revered certain values. They are called the *virtues.*[43] They have been attributed to wise men, holy men, saints and gods. They have made the difference between a barbarian and a cultured person, the difference between chaos and a decent society.

---

43. Virtues: The ideal qualities in good human conduct.

It doesn't absolutely require a heavenly mandate nor a tedious search through the thick tomes of the philosophers to discover what "good" is. A self-revelation can occur on the subject.

It can be worked out by almost any person.

If one were to think over how he or she would like
to be treated by others, one would evolve the
human virtues. Just figure out how you
would want people to treat *you*.

You would possibly, first of all, want to be treated *justly:* you wouldn't want people lying about you or falsely or harshly condemning you. Right?

You would probably want your friends and companions to be *loyal:* you would not want them to betray you.

You could want to be treated with
good sportsmanship,
not hoodwinked nor tricked.

You would want people to be *fair* in
their dealings with you.

You would want them to be *honest* with you
and not cheat you. Correct?

You might want to be treated *kindly*
and without cruelty.

You would possibly want people to be *considerate*
of your rights and feelings.

When you were down, you might like others
to be *compassionate.*

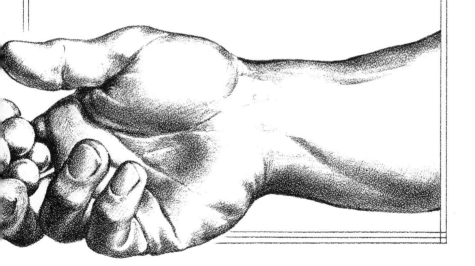

Instead of blasting you, you would probably want others to exhibit *self-control.* Right?

If you had any defects or shortcomings, if you made a mistake, you might want people to be *tolerant,* not critical.

Rather than concentrating on censure and punishment, you would prefer people were *forgiving*. Correct?

You might want people to be *benevolent* toward you, not mean nor stingy.

Your possible desire would be for others to
believe in you, not doubt you
at every hand.

You would probably prefer to be given *respect,*
not insulted.

Possibly you would want others to be *polite* to you and also treat you with *dignity.* Right?

You might like people to *admire* you.

When you did something for them you would
possibly like people to *appreciate* you.
Correct?

You would probably like others to be *friendly*
toward you.

From some you might want *love*.

And above all, you wouldn't want these people just
pretending these things, you would want them to
be quite real in their attitudes and to be
acting with *integrity*.

You could probably think of others. And there are the precepts contained in this book. And you would have worked out the summary of what are called the *virtues*.

It requires no great stretch of imagination for one to recognize that if he were to be treated that way regularly by others around him, his life would exist on a pleasant level. And it is doubtful if one would build up much animosity toward those who treated him in this fashion.

There is an interesting phenomenon[44] at work in human relations. When one person yells at another, the other has an impulse to yell back. One is treated pretty much the way he treats others: one actually sets an example of how he should be treated. A is mean to B so B is mean to A. A is friendly to B so B is friendly to A. I am sure you have seen this at work continually. George hates all women so women tend to hate George. Carlos acts tough to everyone so others tend to act tough toward Carlos—and if they don't dare out in the open, they privately may nurse a hidden impulse to act very tough indeed toward Carlos if they were ever to get a chance.

---

44. Phenomenon: An observable fact or event.

In the unreal world of fiction and the motion pictures, one sees polite villains with unbelievably efficient gangs and lone heroes who are outright boors.[45] Life really isn't like that: real villains are usually pretty crude people and their henchman cruder; Napoleon and Hitler were betrayed right and left by their own people. Real heroes are the quietest-talking fellows you ever met and they are very polite to their friends.

---

45. Boor: A person with rude, clumsy manners and little refinement.

When one is lucky enough to get to meet and talk to the men and women who are at the top of their professions, one is struck by an observation often made that they are just about the nicest people you ever met. That is one of the reasons they are at the top: they try, most of them, to treat others well. And those around them respond and tend to treat them well and even forgive their few shortcomings.

All right, one can work out for himself the human virtues just by recognizing how he himself would like to be treated. And from that, I think you will agree, one has settled any confusions as to what "good conduct" really is. It's a far cry from being inactive, sitting still with your hands in your lap and saying nothing. "Being good" can be a very active and powerful activity.

There is little joy to be found in gloomy, restrained solemnity. When some of old made it seem that to practice virtue required a grim and dismal sort of life, they tended to infer that all pleasure came from being wicked: nothing could be further from the facts. Joy and pleasure do *not* come from immorality! Quite the reverse! Joy and pleasure arise only in honest hearts: the immoral lead unbelievably tragic lives filled with suffering and pain. The human virtues have little to do with gloominess.

They are the bright face of life itself.

Now what do you suppose would happen if one were to try to treat those around him with *justness, loyalty, good sportsmanship, fairness, honesty, kindness, consideration, compassion, self-control, tolerance, forgivingness, benevolence, belief, respect, politeness, dignity, admiration, friendliness, love,* and did it with *integrity?*

It might take a while but don't you suppose that many others would then begin to try to treat one the same way?

Even allowing for the occasional lapses—the news that startles one half out of his wits, the burglar one has to bop on the head, the nut who is driving slow in the fast lane when one is late for work—it should be fairly visible that one would lift oneself to a new plane of human relations. One's survival potential would be considerably raised. And certainly one's life would be a happier one.

One *can* influence the conduct of others around him. If one is not doing that already, it can be made much easier to do so by just picking one virtue a day and specializing in it for that day. Doing that, they would all eventually be in.

Aside from personal benefit, one can take a hand,
no matter how small, in beginning a new era
for human relations.

The pebble, dropped in a pool, can make ripples
to the furthest shore.

The way to happiness is made much brighter by applying the precept: "Try to treat others as you would want them to treat you."

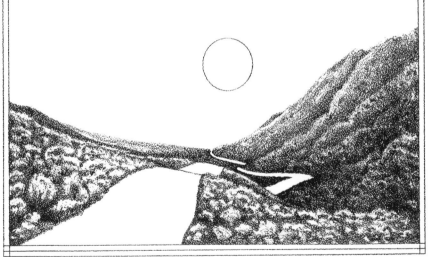

Flourish[46] and Prosper.[47]

Sometimes others seek to crush one down, to make
nothing out of one's hopes and dreams,
one's future and one, himself.

By ridicule and many other means, another who is
evil-intentioned toward one can try
to bring about one's decline.

For whatever reason, efforts to improve oneself,
to become happier in life, can become
the subject of attacks.

---

46. Flourish: To be in a state of activity and production; expanding in influence; thriving; visibly doing well.

47. Prosper: To achieve economic success; succeeding at what one does.

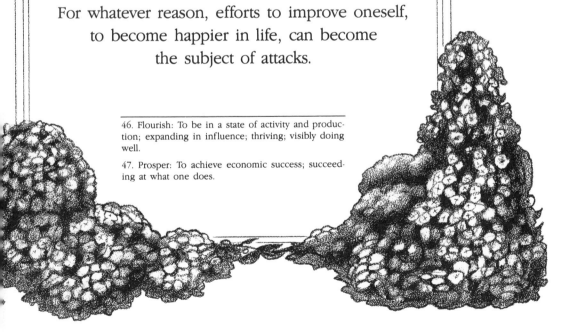

It is sometimes necessary to handle such directly.
But there is a long-range handling
that seldom fails.

What, exactly, are such people trying to do to one?
They are trying to reduce one downward. They
must conceive that one is dangerous to them in
some way: that if one got up in the world, one
could be a menace to them. So, in various ways,
such seek to depress one's talents
and capabilities.

Some madmen even have a general plan that goes like this: "If A becomes more successful, A could be a menace to me; therefore I must do all I can to make A less successful." It never seems to occur to such that their actions might make an enemy out of A even though he was no enemy before. It can be classed as an almost certain way for such madmen to get into trouble. Some do it just from prejudice or because they "don't like someone."

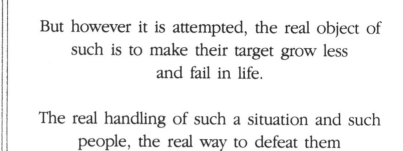

But however it is attempted, the real object of
such is to make their target grow less
and fail in life.

The real handling of such a situation and such
people, the real way to defeat them
is to flourish and prosper.

Oh, yes, it is true that such people, seeing one improve his lot, can become frantic and attack all the harder. The thing to do is handle them if one must but don't give up flourishing and prospering for that is what such people want you to do.

If you flourish and prosper more and more,
such people go into apathy about it;
they can give it up completely.

If one's aims in life are worthwhile, if one carries
them out with some attention to the precepts in this
book, if one flourishes and prospers, one certainly
will wind up the victor. And, hopefully, without
harming a single hair on their heads.

And that is my wish for you:
flourish and prosper!

Epilogue.

Happiness lies in engaging in worthwhile activities.
But there is only one person who for certain can tell
what will make one happy—oneself.

The precepts given in this book are really the edges
of the road: violating them, one is like the motorist
who plunges onto the verge—the result
can be wreckage of the moment,
the relationship, a life.

Only you can say where the road goes for one sets
his goals for the hour, for the relationship,
for the phase of life.

One can feel at times like a spinning leaf blown
along a dirty street, one can feel like a grain of sand
stuck in one place. But nobody has said that life
was a calm and orderly thing; it isn't. One isn't
a tattered leaf nor a grain of sand: one can,
to a greater or lesser degree, draw
his road map and follow it.

One can feel that things are such now that it is much too late to do anything, that one's past road is so messed up that there is no chance of drawing a future road that will be any different: there is always a point on the road when one can map a new one. And try to follow it. There is no person alive who cannot make a new beginning.

It can be said without the slightest fear of con-
tradiction that others may mock one and seek by
various means to push one onto the verge, to tempt
one in various ways to lead an immoral life: all such
persons do so to accomplish private ends of their
own and one will wind up, if one heeds them,
in tragedy and sorrow.

Of course one will have occasional losses trying to apply this book and get it applied. One should just learn from these and carry on. Who said the road doesn't have bumps? It can still be traveled. So people can fall down: it doesn't mean they can't get up again and keep going.

If one keeps the edges on the road, one can't go
far wrong. True excitement, happiness
and joy come from other things,
not from broken lives.

If you can get others to follow the road, you yourself
will be free enough to give yourself a chance
to discover what real happiness is.

The way to happiness is a high-speed road
to those who know where the edges are.

You're the driver.

Fare well.

Join the campaign for
a happier world.

Distribute
The Way To Happiness
Pocket-sized booklets.

You are important to other people.
You are listened to.
You can influence others.

The happiness or unhappiness of others you could
name is important to you.

Without too much trouble, using this book, you
can help them survive and lead happier lives.

The Way To Happiness is available to you in beautiful pocket-sized booklets, to give away to your friends, family and acquaintances. These booklets are available in packs of 12 only, at a cost of $9.00 per pack of 12. Ask about special bulk discounts for schools, groups and organizations.

Additional copies of this hardback edition can also be ordered direct from the publisher for $13.95.

Order today from:
Bridge Publications, Inc.
1414 North Catalina Street
Los Angeles, CA 90027

If ordering by credit card enclose type of card, number, expiration date and signature.

The Way To Happiness is being distributed all over the world in many languages to help create more honesty, trust and happiness. To find out more about The Way To Happiness Campaign and how you can help, contact:

The Way To Happiness Foundation
3540 Wilshire Boulevard, Suite 320
Los Angeles, CA 90010
(213) 738-5096

This may be the first nonreligious moral code based wholly on common sense. It was written by L. Ron Hubbard as an individual work and is not part of any religious doctrine. Any reprinting or individual distribution of it does not infer connection with or sponsorship of any religious organization. It is therefore admissable for government departments and employees to distribute it as a nonreligious activity.
(Reprinting can be arranged with the copyright owner
or his personal representatives.)

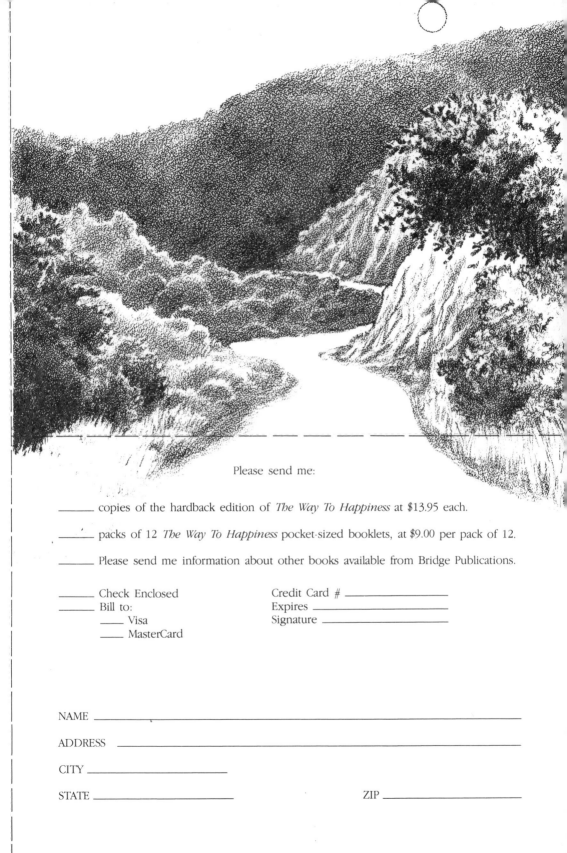

Please send me:

_____ copies of the hardback edition of *The Way To Happiness* at $13.95 each.

_____ packs of 12 *The Way To Happiness* pocket-sized booklets, at $9.00 per pack of 12.

_____ Please send me information about other books available from Bridge Publications.

_____ Check Enclosed   Credit Card # _____
_____ Bill to: Expires _____
    _____ Visa   Signature _____
    _____ MasterCard

NAME _____

ADDRESS _____

CITY _____

STATE _____   ZIP _____

BUSINESS REPLY CARD
FIRST CLASS   PERMIT No. 62688   LOS ANGELES, CALIF.

POSTAGE WILL BE PAID BY ADDRESSEE

Bridge Publications, Inc.
1414 North Catalina Street
Los Angeles, CA 90027

I would like more information about The Way To Happiness
Foundation, what is being done to distribute
The Way To Happiness internationally,
and how I can help.

NAME _____

ADDRESS _____

CITY _____ STATE _____ ZIP _____

BUSINESS REPLY MAIL
FIRST CLASS PERMIT NO. 65103 LOS ANGELES, CA

POSTAGE WILL BE PAID BY ADDRESSEE

The Way To Happiness Foundation
3540 Wilshire Boulevard, Suite 320
Los Angeles, CA 90010